Bette Bo
Mark Rav

A Life in Three Acts

Methuen Drama

Published by Methuen Drama 2009

1 3 5 7 9 10 8 6 4 2

Methuen Drama
A & C Black Publishers Limited
36 Soho Square
London W1D 3HB
www.acblack.com

ISBN: 978 1 4081 2521 2

A CIP catalogue record for this book is available
from the British Library

Typeset by Country Setting, Kingsdown, Kent
Printed and bound in Great Britain by
CPI Cox & Wyman, Reading, Berkshire

BETTE BOURNE
MARK RAVENHILL

A Life in Three Acts

This production opened
at the Traverse Theatre, Edinburgh,
on 18 August 2009

18–30 August, Traverse Theatre, Edinburgh
2–6 September, Koninklijke Schouwburg,
The Hague (Dutch premiere)
21–27 September, Soho Theatre, London

Produced by London Artists Projects in association with
Koninklijke Schouwburg / Het Paradijs, The Hague (NL)

A Life in Three Acts

Bette Bourne
Mark Ravenhill

Direction	**Mark Ravenhill**
Producer	**Jeremy Goldstein**
Picture Editor	**Sheila Corr**
Company Stage Manager	**Sarah Tryfan**
Production Consultant	**Jamie Maisey**

PRESS

Edinburgh	**Liz Smith**
	0797 141 7210 daisyben@msn.com
London	**Sharon Kean**
	0797 384 3133 sharon@keanlanyon.com

INTERNET FILM

Bette Bourne
Mark Ravenhill

Young Bette	**Chris Cookson**
Writer/Director	**Helen Wickham**
Costume	**Maria Jo Garcia**
Make Up	**Paul Shaw**
Camera	**Graham Cantwell**
	Richard York
	Hannan Majid
Still Photography	**Åsa Johannesson**

Thanks to Department of Drama, Queen Mary, University of London; Dawkins Colour, London; Mel Kenyon; and Mair Davies

Bette Bourne

Bette Bourne founded and toured worldwide with his legendary OBIE Award winning queer theatre company, Bloolips. In 1995 he won a Manchester Evening News Award for his performance as Lady Bracknell in *The Importance of Being Earnest* (English Touring Theatre), a credit he also shares with Quentin Crisp. His incarnation as Quentin Crisp in Tim Fountain's *Resident Alien* (Bush Theatre, New York Theatre Workshop, Sydney Gay and Lesbian Mardi Gras and on tour around the world) has been highly successful and brought an entirely new perspective and audience to his work. Over the past decade Bette has also worked with Neil Bartlett and Nick Bloomfield's company *Gloria*, appearing in their production of *Sarasine*, and as Gower in *Pericles* which Neil Bartlett directed for Lyric Hammersmith. Other noted roles include Dogberry in *Much Ado About Nothing* (RSC), Meredith Mayhew in *Theatre of Blood* (Improbable/National Theatre), and Pauncefort Quentin in *The Vortex* (Donmar Warehouse) for which he won the Clarence Derwent Award. More recently, Bette played leading roles in *Deep Rimming in Poplar*, and *Rock* (London Artists Projects/Bette Bourne Company), both of which were written for him by Tim Fountain. With Mark Ravenhill, Bette performed as Queen Victoria in *Ripper* (Union Theatre).

Mark Ravenhill

Mark Ravenhill's first play *Shopping and Fucking* was produced by Out Of Joint and the Royal Court Theatre. Followed by *Faust is Dead* and *Handbag* (ATC) and *Some Explicit Polaroids* (Out Of Joint), *Mother Clap's Molly House* (National Theatre/West End), *Totally Over You* at the National in 2003. Other plays include his one-man show *Product* (Edinburgh Festival Fringe, Royal Court Theatre and European tour), *The Cut* (Donmar), *Citizenship* (National Theatre 2006/2007), *Pool (No Water)* (Frantic Assembly/Lyric Hammersmith) and Mark's pantomime *Dick Whittington and His Cat* at the Barbican Centre. His award winning epic cycle of short plays, *Ravenhill for Breakfast* (Paines Plough) opened at the Edinburgh Festival Fringe in 2007 where Mark received a Spirit of the Festival Award. In 2008 the Gate Theatre, National Theatre, Out of Joint, Paines Plough, the Royal Court and BBC Radio 3 joined forces to individually produce and present the plays together entitled *Shoot/Get Treasure/Repeat*. In 2009, Mark's new play *Over There* opened at the Royal Court Theatre and was subsequently performed at the Schaubühne in Berlin, in a production, co-directed by Mark with Ramin Gray. In November, Mark's adaptation of Terry Pratchett's *Nation* will open in the Olivier Theatre at the National Theatre, London.

Jeremy Goldstein

Jeremy is the founder and executive director of London Artists Projects, a company he has built from scratch, turning it into a leading independent producer of contemporary arts projects. Prior to forming London Artists Projects, Jeremy worked with a number of arts organisations in the UK and Australia including ICA, Southbank Centre, LIFT and Sydney Festival. In 1988, with the Assistance of an Australia Council grant, he trained as a producer with the Australian Elizabethan Theatre Trust (now Performing Lines) touring large-scale ambitious projects all over the world.

Sheila Corr

Sheila Corr has worked in publishing for over 30 years, predominantly for illustrated magazine and book publishers, usually starting from a basic text to seek out suitable pictures in personal, public and commercial archives on subjects ranging from boxing to the Cold War. She has worked closely with authors to illustrate a number of autobiographies, and is fascinated by creating a visual sense of time and place. Sheila has done some television research on *What the Papers Say* with Don McCullin, but this is her theatrical debut.

Sarah Tryfan

Sarah trained at RADA. Recent theatre includes: *Over There, The Stone, The Ugly One*, Mark Ravenhill's *Birth of a Nation, The Arsonists* (Royal Court), *Mine* (Shared Experience), *I'll Be The Devil* (RSC), *King of Hearts* (Out of Joint). Recent opera includes: *Norma, Falstaff, L'elisir d'amore* (Grange Park Opera).

London Artists Projects

London Artists Projects is an organisation committed to commissioning, producing, and managing contemporary arts projects.

Our artist-clients are those who pursue new directions and open up previously unexplored territory to satisfy audiences who hunger for the live and authentic moments of joy, beauty, and meaning that crystallise, reflect and add to their understanding and knowledge of today's world.

Since 2001, London Artists Projects has nurtured and produced a number of seminal projects in the UK and abroad generating revenues in excess of £1.5 million. In the last eighteen months, our projects have reached an estimated audience of 250,000 people.

Recent projects include Cardboard Citizens' *Mincemeat* by Adrian Jackson and Farhana Sheikh at Cordy House, London; Jyll Bradley's *Fragrant Project* for Liverpool European Capital of Culture 2008; Tim Hopkins' *Elephant and Castle* opera for Aldeburgh Festival 2007; Rose English's *Ornamental Happiness* for Liverpool Biennial 2006 and *Carnesky's Ghost Train* as the originating producer with Marisa Carnesky 2003-5.

Patron
Richard Jones

Directors
Robert Cogo-Fawcett (Chairman), **Kim Evans OBE**, **Jeremy Goldstein** (Executive Director), **Sarah Hickson**, **Derek Richards**, **Andrew Taylor**, **Anne Torreggiani**

londonartistsprojects.com
info@londonartistsprojects.com

London Artists Projects is a not-for-profit company limited by guarantee. Registration no. 04752365 VAT registration no. 893887151

London Artists Projects is funded by:

Koninklijke Schouwburg

Director **Oscar Wibaut**
Deputy Director **Erik Kouwenhoven**

Koninklijke Schouwburg (The Royal Theatre) in The Hague is one of Holland's leading theatres for classical drama and newly written repertoire, presenting approximately 180 performances per season on its main stage which seats 680 people. Het Nationale Toneel (National Theatre) is the in-house company which also presents performances of four classic or contemporary drama per season (August–June). During the rest of the year the Koninklijke Schouwburg presents the main Dutch theatre companies, opera, cabaret, comedy, children's and youth theatre.

The Koninklijke Schouwburg co-produces and presents international theatre companies from England, France, Belgium, Germany, Russia and India. Cheek by Jowl, the National Theatre, and Out of Joint have all presented their work in The Hague.

Het Paradijs (The Paradise) is the small black box stage which seats 65 people presenting approximately 140 performances per season. Het Paradijs co-produces and presents young national and international theatre focusing on newly written repertoire, and experimental work. Het Paradijs has presented productions from English companies including Filter, Citizens/Tag Theatre, and V.AMP Productions Limited.

A Life in Three Acts is the first co-production with London Artists Projects.

ks.nl

koninklijke
schouwburg

Traverse Theatre

Artistic Director **Dominic Hill**
Administrative Director **Mike Griffiths**

The Traverse is Scotland's New Writing Theatre. From its conception in the 1960s, it has embraced a spirit of innovation and risk-taking that launched the careers of many of Scotland's best-known writers including John Byrne, David Greig, David Harrower and Liz Lochhead. It is a pivotal venue in Edinburgh and receives enormous critical and audience acclaim for its programming, as well as regularly winning awards. In 2009, *Pornography* by Simon Stephens was awarded Best New Play at the Critics Awards for Theatre in Scotland making it the second consecutive win for a Traverse production with Alan Wilkins' *Carthage Must Be Destroyed* picking up the award in 2008. In 2008 the Traverse's Festival programme Manifesto picked up an incredible sixteen awards including a record seven Scotsman Fringe Firsts and four Herald Angels.

The Traverse's success isn't limited to the Edinburgh stage. Since 2001 Traverse productions have toured not only within Scotland and the UK, but in Sweden, Norway, the Balkans, the Middle East, Germany, USA, Iran, Jordan and Canada. In 2009 the Traverse toured its production of *Midsummer* by David Greig and Gordon McIntyre to Ireland and Canada.

traverse.co.uk

Soho Theatre

Artistic Director **Lisa Goldman**
Executive Director **Mark Godfrey**

- Produces new work
- Discovers and nurtures new writers
- Targets and develops new audiences

Soho Theatre creates and enables daring and original new work that challenges the status quo by igniting the imaginations of writers, artists and audiences. We initiate new conversations with London and the wider world through projects that celebrate creative participation, internationalism and freedom of expression. We nurture a socially and culturally broad audience for theatre and create a buzz around theatre as a living and relevant art form.

'A home to radical international drama'
New Statesman

Soho Theatre Bar
Our bar serves tasty and affordable food and drink from 11am until 11pm Monday-Saturday. The bar is open later to ticketholders (11.30pm Monday-Thursday, 12pm Friday-Saturday).

Soho Theatre Online
For regular email updates, sign up at sohotheatre.com/mailing list, or find us on facebook, twitter, myspace and YouTube.

sohotheatre.com

Introduction

For most of my existence, I never really cared much for life stories. From time to time, I'd buy a biography of a famous novelist or playwright. But I'd always go straight to the index, look up the books or plays the famous author had written and then read only those pages of the biography. The bits in between – the relationships, the personal struggles and (most tedious of all) the childhood – never really had any interest for me.

When my dad retired a few years ago, he decided to devote a lot of his time to researching the family tree. I watched with puzzled amusement as he drove up and down the country hunting for obscure parish registers, trying to piece together a story for himself. It clearly meant a lot to him; I really couldn't see the appeal.

Around this time, a friend invited me to take part in an arts project she was organising in Germany. Video booths were set up and people were invited to tell their life stories, which were then transmitted to an audience in an adjacent room. Guests could talk for as long as they liked: some people gave a concise ten-minute summary of their lives while others talked for hours, recalling their pasts in precise detail.

I was all set to take part in the German event but then at the last minute I cancelled. With a shock of self-realisation, I recognised that I was too scared to go and sit in a video booth and tell the story of my life. This troubled me for months. After all, there wasn't some traumatic past experience that I was frightened to talk about. My life had been one of the most serene, even banal lives that I could possibly imagine. Maybe it was this: that I was worried that my life was just too boring. This could be the reason that I was avoiding telling my own life story and why I found published biographies so dull. But only partly. There was some other reason for my own fear that I couldn't quite locate and so, a couple of years ago, I decided to confront my fear.

One day, I got some large sheets of paper and I wrote a list of years along the bottom, starting with 1966 (the year I was born) and on to the present day. I then spent the day filling in as much as I could remember beside each year – writing scene headings, key words, little snatches of remembered speech. It was an illuminating experience – and one that I would recommend to anyone. Suddenly, connections and echoes were revealed to me, patterns which I'd never noticed before. Seen in this context, things that I'd blamed myself for – or other people – seemed totally understandable. I was able to look back with a forgiveness that I'd never felt before. Far from being a frightening or dull experience, piecing my life together like this had actually been an illuminating and ultimately rather comforting experience.

It's ironic then that only a few months after this I suffered a significant loss of memory. I had been epileptic for over a decade but one night I suffered an enormous seizure. I was in hospital in a state of coma for several days. Doctors warned my parents that I might not recover at all and if I did that I could be severely brain-damaged, with profound amnesia. They were wrong. In fact, I made a swift recovery. To the doctors' surprise, I knew exactly who I was and recognised all the friends and family members who came to visit me in the hospital.

But then I discovered that I'd lost all memory of the events of the three weeks leading up to the attack. Looking through my diary I could see a list of events for this period and I found theatre and cinema tickets, receipts for meals eaten and taxis taken. None of them triggered any mental pictures at all.

At first I was dismissive of this memory loss. Friends said, 'Isn't it traumatic to forget like this?' But I said, 'It's only a few weeks, what possible harm can that do?' and I carried on with my life.

Gradually, though, I found myself more and more troubled by those missing few weeks. The feeling that my life had a gap in it – and with it my existence, my identity – was giving me a sense of incompleteness about myself, a nagging sense that there was a version of me who had gone through several weeks of an existence which I would never know. I realised that a concrete, linear sense of life, of small and big experiences following one after the other, is essential to forming a sense of who we are. Now that my seizure had ripped a few pages out of the book of my life I began to appreciate just how important and powerful our biographies can be. I had a renewed hunger for life stories.

Then I remembered my first meeting with Bette Bourne. In 2000, I was running a workshop at the National Theatre Studio for my play *Mother Clap's Molly House*, trying to find some purchase on the extraordinary gay history of early eighteenth-century London. A friend of mine recommended Bette, who I'd seen being very good in Neil Bartlett's *Sarassine*. Bette turned out to be a very reluctant improviser but one day he suddenly said to the actors in the room: 'Oh this bit reminds me of the time that I was living in the drag commune.' I was instantly eager to hear more and we stopped our impro for the afternoon while Bette told us the incredible social and sexual adventure of the commune he'd been involved with in 1970s Notting Hill.

Since that workshop, I've been in pretty much constant contact with Bette, who has gradually told me about more of the incidents of his life. I realised that he had led a life with great personal strength and bravery, but also that he'd been involved in a political and social struggle from which I had benefited enormously.

In 2006, we were asked to talk about Bette's life on the stage of the Vauxhall Tavern as part of gay history month. In our twenty-minute slot I played the 'straight' man prompting Bette to tell the story of the commune to an enthusiastic, mostly drunk audience. It was an exciting event: a new generation of gay men and women were discovering a story that mattered to them.

I realised that Bette's life needed far more than twenty minutes. I wanted to give it the space to unfold over time, something quite different from the short chat-show slots which are our usual public forum for talking about celebrated lives. I thought about writing a book, a conventional biography of Bette's story. But after our Vauxhall Tavern experience, I realised that it was a story that had to be told onstage: to get the essence of Bette we needed to see him showing off, singing and telling stories. But also we needed to see the moments in which the mask slips to reveal the vulnerability but also the anger which is very much part of Bette Bourne.

I asked Bette to meet with me over a period of a few weeks and talk me through his life. I recorded these conversations and they were transcribed. I shaped and edited them, but tried to keep something of the hesitations and the repetitions of our conversations. It is these edited transcripts that are published here – an attempt to recreate an intimate conversation between friends for a paying public.

There are many aspects of Bette's story that are still not much talked about, despite our supposedly liberated age: the hidden life of gay men in the 1950s with its particular fears and exhilarations, the incredible sudden rush of consciousness-raising that Gay Lib brought in the early 1970s and, in the third act of our piece, the experience of growing old as a gay man. I find Bette's story moving and inspiring and I hope others will too. It's taken me a while but I've now come to realise just how important a biography can be.

Mark Ravenhill
July 2009

A Life in Three Acts

Characters

Mark
Bette

Act One

Mark Hello, I'm Mark Ravenhill. I'm a playwright. In the past few weeks, I've been talking to the performer Bette Bourne about his life. We've divided our conversation into three parts. A life in three acts. Tonight is part one. We'd like to read you edited transcripts of our conversations. Ladies, gentlemen and all others – Bette Bourne.

Bette I was in a group. Madame Behenna and her Dancing Children.

I was four and they dressed me up – this was in the wartime when all the soldiers were away and all the wives came, they were the audience and I was put in a miniature air force suit and I was pushing a big pram on to the stage but the pram was like much taller than me and there was this little girl and I sang.

I was very very tiny but I had a very big voice so it was hilarious people were just wetting themselves laughing. My mother was saying 'That's my son up there!', her bosom swelling of course.

My mother was a real live wire. She was married to this man who was disappointed, bitter, a man who'd been through this hideous war. You see none of us were ever bombed, there were bombs around, there was danger but my mother never experienced it like that. If she was afraid, she would never let us be afraid. She said, 'Quick, the bombs, get under the bed!' And we'd all get under this big double bed that they slept in and the plaster and bricks would all fall on the bed. Even if the roof came in we were sensibly protected by this iron bedstead. And she was very animal like that, very much looking after her kids. She was a very wonderful mother. A wonderful mother. Later on it was more difficult of course, especially when I was out in public. She didn't like any of that at all, she couldn't bear it. She wanted me to have children and carry on the name. She was a real breeder and she still is at ninety-one, she's still wondering when I'm gonna get married and I'm nearly seventy – it's fucking mad! Completely potty. But, see we had a wonderful time.

My dad was in the navy during the war and had a ghastly time and he was very angry all the time I seem to remember. He was a very bright man who ran away from home to the navy and then escaped from the navy and then went back into the navy when the war started and they put him on the minesweepers on the Atlantic which was really, I mean imagine, terrifying, terrifying . . . every minute of the day you expected to be blown up. He came out of the navy practically with white hair. The shock of it.

When we were children you see, my mother would buy all these gifts and that would make my dad very angry but at Christmas time we had to go in and thank him for the gifts and then we'd have the opening all the presents and going in to thank him then he'd say

Dad   'Alright, you boys, off to the park, out you go!'

Bette   He didn't want us in the house at all. He wasn't really interested in children, much to his surprise and chagrin I imagine. But he er . . . no . . . no . . . you were constantly afraid of him and if I did anything really bad my mother would say I'm going to tell Daddy and then she'd tell him and I'd get a very serious warning or he'd give me a good belting. He didn't belt me often but when he did I was thrashed with a cane, a big cane and the cane ended up completely shattered at one point and then he could be very cruel but it wasn't often, but when it was it was like a huge thunderstorm it was terrifying. And I was terrified of him for most of my life until I got my frock on!

Mark   So that was . . .

Bette   That was much later.

Mark   One of the first things I was thinking of asking you next was, we are all of us given some basic messages about life from our parents: things that are right, things that are wrong, things that we should be scared of, and I was going to say to you what do you think the basic messages about life that you got from your mother and father were?

Bette   An enormous cheerfulness from my mother, an enormous feeling that life was great and there were lots of exciting things. And she was one of the people who helped by getting me into drama school. You want to be an actor? OK let's deal with that. He said to me

Dad   'You want to be an actor? You tell me about being a fucking actor when you're at the Old Vic earning £35 a week!'

Bette   Well I got to the Old Vic and I was making a lot more than £35 a week and I invited him to the show. And he wouldn't come. He met me in a cafe nearby and he wouldn't come. And we talked about this before and he wouldn't come. I mean he was afraid of the whole middle-class thing of the Old Vic. That was what he was really afraid of but he would not pick up that ticket off the table and say thanks, well done. My fucking doctor from where I lived in Green Lanes came with his wife and afterwards he said, 'I saw you at the Old Vic last night, jolly good, jolly good. You did it!' And he made me feel you did it. It was enormous achievement for me, coming from fucking Hackney with everyone saying 'Nah not for you. You get a job in the post office delivering telegrams, delivering letters.' That's what a lot of the lads did. I actually got my father, my father was actually a great help at getting me into the printing trade at the beginning.

It's very emotional stuff isn't it?

Mark   Yes. But why do you make your mum and your dad . . . do you want tissues?

Bette   No it was just suddenly . . . (*Upset.*)

Mark   Do you want some bog roll? No it is very emotional. But you make your mum and your dad sound so different? Why were they together?

Bette   Sense of humour. A great sense of humour and they were both very good-looking, very beautiful young people. He was an extremely handsome young man, he looked like Rory Calhoun or something, an English version. And my mother looked like this absolute beauty. She had this wonderfully pure look almost angelic. And they were both sex mad which was a great link. They had lots of sex.

Mark   And when did you become aware of that?

Bette   She told me later . . . Aware of that?

Mark   I mean how soon is a kid aware of their parents having sex?

Bette   I mean you'd hear them laughing on a Sunday morning, and him lying in bed tickling her, them shrieking and screaming and then you'd hear the sounds of passion and then you know. I mean that was the day off when they really enjoyed each other. He had horrible jobs like house painting and decorating and selling tea and selling ice creams at Wembly Stadium, shitty jobs he had.

I got to the secondary modern. But they did teach strange things like typing at my school and metalwork. It was what they called a commercial school. Upton House in Hackney. But I was producing even then. At school. I was producing. First thing I did was *Mr and Mrs Scrooge*. I was eleven and the boy who played Mrs Scrooge was built like a tank, a huge, gorgeous guy. Blond, big blue eyes. And he came on in drag and of course the kids went mad because he was really butch guy, Hugh Wakefield I remember his name was, and then I started laughing, completely broke up but him coming on was just hilarious because he was very cheerful with big sort of sunrise eyes you know? And he had this terrible old wig and he looked like a war worker, a lady war worker, and he'd borrowed one of those double pinnies from his mum that go right round . . . (*Laughing.*)

Mark   And was that the first time that you'd come into contact with somebody in drag like that, the power they could have on an audience?

Bette   He came in like this . . . he was so pleased with himself. Well they just went mad. And he was a sweet guy, a sweet guy, he was having fun. He was just in the fun of it.

So we did that and then we did *Julius Caesar* at the Round Chapel, you know it's now a rock gig in Hackney, just off Mare Street. We just did from the beginning of the play until Act Three, after the stabbing. The stabbing was the end of the show.

I played Julius Caesar, you know I wanted the title role. I just knew that Julius Caesar was the boss.

This tall Jewish lad played Casca, and he said, 'Speak hands for me!' Bang and I was stabbed. The whole school cheered, cheered because this snotty little queen had got her come-uppance. So there were two plays going on, if you see what I mean. (*Laugh.*) Loved it. Had a wonderful time. That was directed by one of the masters. He was called Dicky Windle.

Mark   And were you aware by then of sex, sexuality?

Bette   Oh I was going in the toilets with the lads, with the pretty ones. You see the scripture class was the picking-up place all the queens picked each other up at the scripture class and you'd have a little J Arthur and that would be that. Lovely. (*Laugh.*)

Mark   So that started when, when you went to the secondary school?

Bette   Yeah. It was the beginning . . .

Mark   And was there any religious stuff to all this? It wasn't Catholic?

Bette   No, we had Bible classes but they were usually a big relaxation. Nobody took it seriously. Half the lads were Jewish anyway and weren't interested. And they weren't religious Jews you see they were East End commercial Jews

Mark   So going off to the loos and the J Arthurs, was that pretty guilt-free, fun?

Bette   Yes except one time, I was twelve or thirteen and
Horace Steele said I'll meet you at the Scout Hall at
lunchtime. He had the keys – he was a patrol leader. In the
lunch hour. So I went down there. I was pretty excited you
know. He was a nice lad. I opened the door and she's there
in stockings and suspenders and his mum's bra. He must
have nicked his mum's drag, taken it up in a carrier bag or
something, and he was there ready for me playing this tart.
I was horrified. I was into boys. I wasn't into trannies. I didn't
know what that was about at all. I couldn't believe it. I just
looked. And he'd said come in and I didn't, I wouldn't. I ran.
I turned tail and ran all the way back to school. I was
terrified. Terrified!

No we never spoke after that. It was rather a potent image for
me as you can imagine. My later career.

Mark   So actually, although the 1950s in the history books
were probably the low point for the oppression of gay men,
that wasn't your experience?

Bette   No. We didn't experience it like that, no. No I never
thought about when I was sixteen, seventeen, eighteen,
nineteen. I mean going up to Hampstead Heath and getting
fucked and seeing a policeman coming towards you on a
horse was a lark. You had to run and hide. It was all a lark.
And the whole thing of Polari was a lark, going into the
Vauxhall Tavern when I was seventeen and everybody kind of
polarying away . . . all the gay people on one side and all the
straight people on another.

Mark   So was it something that you just didn't think about,
oh I'm straight or I'm gay.

Bette   I did one day think, I was coming out of the flats in
Green Lanes.

Mark   That's where your family lived?

Bette   Yes, in Amwell Court, it's still there, by the big
reservoir.

And I came out and I'm going up towards Manor House and I notice this boy coming towards me and he had tight white jeans. And I looked at him. And I turned round and looked at his back. And then I realised. Oh that's what I want. Looking at boys. Because I had a girlfriend up the road. I never even tried it on with her. She couldn't understand it. Most working-class boys would have their hands up your knickers first time but I didn't. To me she was like a sister almost. In fact I remember her one day saying to me, 'It's alright, we can do it if you want.' And it had never even occurred to me to feel her up. All the things that most boys did. I wanted those boys. Those males of the species.

Mark   So it sounds like sex, sexuality you never actually felt any fear connected to sex or sexuality in your teenager years?

Bette   Not that you ever thought about it.

Mark   That's great. I think lots of people probably do, even if they're straight.

Bette   I think most of the young queens accepted we were gay, we weren't doing what we were supposed to do, we didn't give a fuck . . . there were plenty of gay clubs all over Soho, all over . . . the Cricketers, the Vauxhall, the Union, the Manor House, gay places all over London, the Duragon. You'd get on the bus and you'd go down there.

Mark   So how did you first know about those places? So you're in the secondary school, you're a kid and you're messing around with the boys at school, but who actually says oh there's pubs and clubs and how do you get there and who takes you there?

Bette   I used to go up to town on a Sunday. I'd get on the 33 tram at Manor House, pay sixpence and it would take you all the way to Westminster, all the way down that tunnel in Holborn . . . you'd get off the tram at Westminster and I'd look at all the great buildings and bridges and walk gradually up past the guards on their horses. Then I'd go into the National Portrait Gallery, look at the pictures. Then I came out and there was this man going past. He had make-up on and bright red hair and a black hat. And I was absolutely horrified. I thought how ghastly. How gross. Of course, it rang a very loud bell. It was Quentin.

Mark   When did you realise it was Quentin Crisp?

Bette   I didn't know who it was.

Then all his stories about Soho and Fitzrovia and so on. But no after I saw him I watched him going up the road, past the Garrick Theatre and up into Soho and I'd heard something about Soho and I don't know what I'd heard but I was looking for someone to interfere with me. And I went up to Old Compton Street and they used to have these Charles Forte American bars, they had these big bays with these counters, you'd get things like milkshakes and coffee, well all that was new. You know, cappuccinos, burgers, and to me that was very exciting that was American, everything American was very big for us after the war because America had saved us. My father didn't think so but we bought it. So it was very exciting and all the film stars and rock 'n' roll people were from there. I remember becoming aware of Elvis Presley when I was at school when I was fourteen, fifteen. We were all getting sticky about Elvis Presley then. So I go into this Charlie Forte's milk bar they were called and you'd just about scrape enough together for a coffee and this man chatted me up he said

Man   'Oh I suppose you want to be an actor.'

Bette   Of course I lit up and said 'Yes, yes I do' and all this stuff. Anyway, he took me up to his flat, took my cherry, gave me a blow job and I felt as if I was just dissolving like a fizzy pill in a glass of water. It was wonderful.

Mark   So what was this man like then? And what was the flat like?

Bette   He was a military man, he was completely bald and he was about in his fifties I suppose.

Mark   God.

Bette   And he took me upstairs and said

Man   'I'm not one of those queers you know.'

Bette   I felt much relieved at that.

Man   'Have you ever been inside a girl?'

Bette   . . . No.

Man   'Well if you'd just lie back a little, I'll show you what it feels like.'

Bette   And I thought well he's not queer. He's showing me something that's marvellous. It never struck me that he was queer, till I got home. I wrote him a long letter telling him I was going to tell the police and everything. Then I tore the letter up and went back next Sunday for another one.

Mark   So you kept in contact with him?

Bette   Yes, I'd go up there every few weeks and ring his bell and he'd invite me up and he'd blow me and that would be that.

Mark   And how long did that last for?

Bette   A few weeks. I mean at the time it feels like a long time but it was probably just a few weeks. And it was funny because he had a picture on his wall, an oil painting, quite a small one of four people, four soldiers clinging to a raft and one of them was bald. And he said to me

Man   'That was me, that's what happened to me during the war. We were blown up and that's me during the war.'

Mark   It was a photo?

Bette   No it was an oil painting. Course it was complete bullshit it was just to get him in the heroic image because we thought soldiers and sailors were marvellous people, they could have anything or do anything. And if you drove a car it was your duty to give a soldier or sailor a lift. My dad used to always cos he was into cars.

Mark   So you were helping out the military . . .

Bette   I was rewarding him! And he told me his name was

Man   Captain Cox

Bette   I've always remembered it.

Mark   So you had this idea of being an actor, but how much did you think about that that would take you away from the jobs that other people were doing?

Bette   Well I had two boyfriends at school, two friends, not sexual and we were together all the time, we went out weekends and eventually I said well I've got to speak posh because I want to be an actor. So I'm going to speak posh from now on. And I was going around speaking posh! And Johnny said

Johnny   'I can't! I can't it's just stupid, I can't listen to all this.'

Bette   And I said, 'Well fuck you. I'm going to be a posh actor and I don't care what you think. Fuck you!' And that was the end of our friendship.

Mark   And how old were you when you started talking posh?

Bette *farts.*

Mark   Bette! This is going to be produced on the world's stages.

Bette *farts three times.*

Mark   And you've got to do that farting every time we do the play.

Bette *laughs.*

Mark   So, how old were you then?

Bette   I was about fourteen, fifteen. Just before I left school and became an apprentice in a printer's. So I had three months of it and then I split, I didn't tell my mum and dad

I got a job in an office. I knew I was going to have to go to drama school, I just knew it.

Mark   And at which stage did you tell your mum and dad that you'd got your grant and got into the drama school?

Bette   Well I'd told them, er . . . I can't remember. I told them I'd got a job in the Garrick Theatre backstage and from earning £2 10 shillings a week I was suddenly earning £15 a week which is enormous for someone of sixteen, seventeen. And that I'd left the print. My father came round . . . because they'd split up by then, I was about sixteen and he said

Dad   'You're mad. That was a job for life. You're so stupid. Why did you do it?'

Bette   Well I want to be an actor.

Dad   Ugh . . .

Bette   So then I went to Central and after that I started working as an actor.

Yes. I had this quite successful little career going and I ended up sort of being the second leading man to Ian McKellen, plays at Edinburgh, and we toured all over the world and we played in London. Erm. And I thought I was the bee's knees. And then I met this guy and we were lovers. Rex. He was a lovely guy. Rex was at art school, at Central. Central St Martin's it's called now, then it was just Central I think. And he was in his last year at the course when I met him. He was a cute, gorgeous, Australian red-haired number and we had a very passionate time.

He hated everything that I was in, that he came to. I was in shows in Ipswich, and Bristol, the Edinburgh Festival with Ian McKellen and all that stuff. And what he meant was we're not really seeing anything of you dear. And looking back I could see what he meant.

And he came in one night and I said, 'Where have you been?' And he said

Rex 'Oh I've been to a meeting.'

Bette What do you mean, a meeting?

Rex 'A political meeting, all these queers.'

Bette What on earth are you talking about? Are you mad? Cos obviously this is my little career trip, soirées, tables and dinner parties, the napkins and all that . . . And he said

Rex 'Oh it's great, there's these gorgeous guys there.'

Bette Well I was there the next Wednesday. I went to the LSE first meeting, the first thing was the sexy boys. First meeting. Mmm mmm lovely. I went along and there were a lot of very beautiful people there. It was all very hippy, meeting people with long hair for the first time and all that sort of stuff. And I sat there and I was pretty conventionally dressed, conventional haircut and all the rest of it. And then I listened to people talking. And then this guy said

Guy 'Well this is just like a fucking gay bar isn't it? We're all just here cruising.'

Bette And I felt this huge eruption of feeling and I was so angry and I stood up and said, 'If you think this is a fucking gay bar you're out of your fucking tree you stupid fucker! We're here talking about our lives about all the things we've never talked about before. We've got a chance. Don't you fucking see, you're stupid!'

There was quite a chill because I'd been very quiet and suddenly all this fishwife was coming out as well you know.

It was a great thing. Great, exciting, thrilling, new, brand new thing. And it was sexy, no. It was wonderful. It was a wonderful moment. And he was trying to cheapen it, trying to make it sound like another cruisy bar up the West End which I knew all about since I was fifteen, sixteen, because I worked in the West End. I was going to all the gay clubs after work. Curtain come down ten o'clock, 10.30 p.m. Pack up. Away. Out. Before even the actors were out. And I was out and up into those gay bars. And I knew all about that. I knew all about the sad queens weeping into their gin, you know all that stuff. And I knew it was a chance. And it was so . . . it was thrilling, it was euphoric.

Mark   So I'm interested in this GLF thing, what surprised me about what you've described so far is that it wasn't that GLF allowed you to express what you felt all along about your life, it was like you looked back over your life and suddenly saw that it was something completely different from what you thought it was.

Bette   Yes.

Mark   That you had actually felt . . .

Bette   Ripped off was how I felt.

Mark   But no only when, I suppose they call it a raising of conciousness, actually you'd felt happy in your life up to that point, as you've told it to me?

Bette   Well I was surprised.

Mark   But where had that come from, because the way you tell me the story, you'd never felt that before . . .

Bette   No but suddenly when you become conscious it affects your whole body.

Mark   I think it's strange there was no . . .

Bette   Lead up?

Mark   Yeah, it's not like the previous two years before you're going round all these gay bars thinking oh there's something missing . . .

Bette   No, never thought that at all.

Mark   There's one life that you completely lived. And then you went to this meeting and saw things completely . . .

Bette   Saw the light.

Mark   Saw things completely differently, that's incredible.

Bette   It's absolutely true. As sure as I'm sitting here talking to you, it was absolutely true. It was thrilling beyond belief and that thrill has lasted almost to this day. It's just I don't have to pretend. I'm out there and I'm queer. I like it up the bum. And fuck you if you don't like that in me.

Mark   And were there some people at that meeting who spoke who particularly inspired you or who you admired?

Bette   What happened after that little explosion of mine, was that someone came rushing up to me and said they wanted me to be on the steering committee. And I said, 'On the what?' I had no idea what a steering committee was, what consciousness-raising . . . I had no idea of any of that. All I knew in my gut was that there was a new feeling in this room, amongst these three hundred men and women, and they were actually trying to talk about things, to discuss things. You'd never talk about that in a gay bar. It was all about the one you'd fucked last week and how big his cock was and where you'd met and are you going to see them again . . . you know. You never asked is he interesting, is he funny. You asked how big was it. It was very much at a meat-market level. And for a newcomer of course, I was pretty very much in shape. I was very much in demand of course I loved it. But then there was something else that hadn't occurred to any of us. And later on I went to gay marches, three hundred thousand people on that march going underneath Charing Cross Bridge, across that bridge. So we'd come from two people at the LSE, Aubrey Walter and David Fernbach, Bob Mellors rather . . . been to New York, picked up the idea there, put a little notice on the board, Gay Liberation Front meeting and I think about seven people turned up. Then it was seventy, then it was seven hundred, then it was seven thousand. I mean it just grew so quickly it was very exciting. Going down the street dressed up, going to the people screaming and shouting, 'It's not like that darling, it's like fairy.' I had a great anger in me. This queen was coming up, the crown of the queen was coming up, that's very strong you see. I made a complete fool of myself.

Mark   You haven't stopped yet . . .

Bette   I haven't stopped no! It's absolutely true.

Mark   But coming out of that meeting did that have an immediate effect on you the next day, the way you dealt with people you were working with, your family?

Bette   Well we all went down to the bar afterwards and had a drink, and there were obviously one or two people that I knew from the gay scene and Ramsey this guy I knew, and various people I knew, and some of the people I had known carnally and urm that was nice. And then we went home, gradually we got this thing called consciousness-raising together, and then we got demonstrations, walking down Oxford Street in all these wild costumes, feathers and make-up and stuff. Very street theatre. And the famous riot in Grosvenor Square was around that time. The Industrial Relations Bill. Edward Heath. Red Ladder had started and they were marvellous. There was this huge thing for the coal miners at Hyde Park Corner and Red Ladder brought this huge red ladder, it was huge, and they went right up to the top and they did a show. I think the show was about two minutes. And it was like 'We don't want a slice, we want the fucking bakery!' And everybody cheered and they got down and went into another part of the crowd, it was thrilling beyond words. There were these literally thousands of miners were there, queens were there. It was the beginning of a lot of different theatre things at that time.

Mark   But away from the meetings, in the first few days or whatever, did that change your day-to-day life?

Bette   Yes we sat around each other's flats. I opened up my flat. And people would come by and look for crash pads, and you'd put people up. And it all became you know, a very different life. I never went for any auditions. They were always interested in what was going on in what I liked to call the fucking straight theatre. And there was a street theatre that I became part of but I didn't think that that was that interesting.

Mark   So that was a big change, so if we'd taken a photo of you in 1969 you would have been in a kind of conventional sixties suit, conventional hair, and then if we'd taken a photo of you in 1970 . . .

Bette   Longish hair. This kind of length. But eventually I had hair down to here.

Mark   But if we'd taken a photo of you in 1971 . . .

Bette   Completely different.

Mark   Right.

Bette   I've got pictures, completely different.

Mark   And was that more or less an overnight change of clothes, did you suddenly throw out the suits?

Bette   Well yeah, I remember saying to Rex, we got involved, and I went to the meeting, and one time he took me to a party and I smoked a bit of spliff. He'd done a bit of that smoke stuff before and I hadn't and he'd kind of been keeping an eye on me. There was an element in our relationship where he was sort of looking after me even though I was much bigger and stronger than he was, physically. I always thought of him as smarter than me, brighter than me because he'd been to university and he'd been to art school and all the rest of it. And he was at great pains to say that wasn't so but it was how I felt. You can't just erase those feelings. And I remember him saying

Rex   'Well I think we should chuck out all this furniture.'

Bette   I had these smart little Victorian chairs, smart little round tables and cabinets. None of it meant anything to me, it just looked a right sort of home for an actor. We got rid of it all. Got the cushions in. Sat on the floor . . . had some dope . . . did acid. A complete change. And it was wonderful.

I had been in drag through GLF and one day I wrote to my dad, I don't know why, I had a strong urge to write to him and to repair things in some way and he said

Dad   'Well shall we meet in a pub?'

Bette   And I said no, I think you should see the jewel in its
setting. So he came to the house and I was wearing drag, I
had little you know, matador pants and little gold shoes with a
sixties heel and I had a little top tucked in at the waist. I had a
great figure at that time. And a lot of long red hennaed hair
and a lot of make-up, full make-up. And when he saw me at
the door I came all the way down from my second-floor flat
and opened the door and there he was in this old raincoat
and he literally shrivelled like a sort of autumn leaf, he backed
off because I put my arms around out to welcome him and he
backed away. And I said, 'Well do you want some tea? Why
don't you come on upstairs?' So he came upstairs and I made
tea. And I said, 'Well I wanted you to see me as I am. And I
wanted to tell you I'm not afraid of you. I think you're a shit.
I think you've been absolutely evil to me. And you're violent
and you beat the shit out of me when I was young . . . ' And
he was terrified, he'd never seen a beautiful queen, let alone
the fact that I was his son. I was in drag. I was a queen.
A beautiful queen.

Act Two

Mark I'm Mark Ravenhill. I'm a playwright. In the past few weeks, I've been talking to the performer Bette Bourne about his life. We've divided our conversation into three parts. A life in three acts. Tonight is part two. We'd like to read you edited transcripts of our conversations. Ladies, gentlemen and all others – Bette Bourne.

Bette I wasn't in drag at the beginning of gay lib.

I had been brought up very butch, and I'd gone to a very butch school and all the rest of it, and that was very important that I was . . . you know that I had that image together. I'd been playing my young Italianate sort of thugs on television in *The Saint, The Baron, Dixon of Dock Green* and all these programmes when I was always the criminal. A sort of East End lad.

I went to Gay Lib thinking I was Che Guevara, and I was dressed like him, and I had a big beard. And I was very butch and I had these boots which were actually too big for me. Boots were too big.

Well one day this queen came in. This queen came into the meeting. She was called Piggy and she was a very interesting art queen, and she was in . . . wearing a denim skirt. And everyone was having little titters, you know, behind their hands and he said

Piggy 'I don't want to be put down by you lot because I'm wearing a skirt. I like my skirt and it's just part of me and if you don't like it you can fuck off! Er . . . but I like it and I don't see why I should have you lot putting me down . . . er . . . for wearing a skirt because I'm a man.'

Bette He was quite, quite a man. And then the next week, the change and the meetings were suddenly over here in the Church Hall and my friend Gordon Howie came round and . . . I was talking about dressing and I said I've got this marvellous dress in the market. And he said

Gordon   'Alright then put it on.'

Bette   So I put it on and he said

Gordon   'Why don't we go over to the Gay Lib meeting?'

Bette   Well I said it's cobbles down there and very difficult to walk. (*Laughter*.) So I got my heels on, got the make-up on, and I looked very pretty. It was a scarlet dress, 1930s cut, and a cut dress . . . So I'm doing . . . I'm walking along with a beautiful Victorian cape and a handbag and I went over to the Gay Lib meeting and sat down. Nobody recognised me at all, they just thought 'Who's this person coming in here and talking and stuff?' So I sat and suddenly felt very relaxed and enjoyed being in my drag because it was like a release.

Yeah, and one or two other queens got into a bit of drag, you know with the dresses and stuff, but it wasn't very many of us, but by the time we moved here, and I went over there, I suppose there was half a dozen of us in drag. But I was the last person they expected . . .

It made me feel a million dollars. I felt so confident . . . and it changed the premise you see. When I was talking about it I wasn't talking about it in the same premise. They were all talking theory and . . . all these American revolutionaries who had, you know, had said this and said that, and written this and written that, you know, um . . . and my thing was I felt completely different. And I started to understand how some of the women might have felt. Just going up the street in a frock was a very different experience − you felt very vulnerable in a way. I was vulnerable in the streets. I got to the Gay Lib meeting and then suddenly my confidence came up because it was all queers and dykes . . . and er it was very nice . . . and I started saying things, you know, to these blokes like, 'Well you've got a lot to say for yourself haven't you?' 'Why don't you give your arse a chance?' You know. And all this cockney fishwife came out (*laughter*) while in an elegant thirties gown.

Mark   And do you think you found out more about yourself through those encountery sessions, all those conscious . . . and were you starting to come to a new idea of who you were?

Bette   Yeah, the Bette Bourne . . .

Mark   Yeah where did that come from?

Bette   That was great. That all started with a couple of queens calling me Bette because it was alliterative. I think it was one queen in particular that started it and . . . er . . . I liked it a lot . . . And er . . .

Mark   Why did you like it?

Bette   I dunno . . . it felt right . . . that with the frock. It felt . . . it felt right. It felt as though . . . I could let go of something.

Well, then gradually more and more people started wearing dresses and then there was a whole group of us that sort of gradually gravitated towards each other, and one day we got really fed up with the meetings and so we decided to go and find somewhere else where we could just all be together in our frocks. So we climbed over the back wall . . . and down the wall into the back garden where this film studio was . . . quite a big film studio building and er . . . and it was like a big hall really, and it was all padded because it had been a sound-proofed film studio, and it was at the end of Colville Gardens, Colville Houses, which is a cul-de-sac. There was a little garden at the front and er . . . we . . . we squatted it.

We moved in and we did it up and we had one end was the Arabian room and as you can imagine it was all bits of schmutter and silk and stuff draped like a tent all along. Then the next room was where the wardrobe was, which was, you know, like that . . . to the wall – that area – and that was hundreds of frocks that we found on the Portobello and stuff. Then the next part was all shoes, about four hundred pairs of shoes. And you could go in and wear what you wanted. There was a mirror . . . you know, you didn't get started until two in the afternoon.

I mean there were silk scarves and beautiful drapes everywhere – all cheap tat, but to us it was fabulous. It was like living in this extraordinary kind of fairylike cocoon. And we all had different drag on every day. Some people changed their drag three times a day. There was a lot of swishing about in drag. Occasionally one would do a bit of ironing. Then we'd have the music on, we'd sit there and listen to Maria Callas all evening, you know, and on the acid and the dope. It was a sort of madness really but it was a great madness. Then there was the office where all the practical stuff took place.

Mark   What practical stuff?

Bette   Well, you know, putting together for instance an issue of *Come Together* which was the gay newspaper which we got, you know, various people in the gay movement . . . there was the women's edition and the drag queens' and the common edition and people wrote articles for it. And that was the sort of thing that went on in the office. Oh . . . one of the things that happened – I was thinking about bills that had to be paid.

Mark   How many people were living there?

Bette   Er, twelve.

Mark   Right.

Bette   There were about nine men, three women and a couple of kids.

Mark   Right.

Bette   And er . . .

Mark   So what was the kind of average day, if there was such a thing?

Bette   Well, you'd wake up about, I suppose, eleven or something . . . and there was a very beautiful queen who always used to get up early and walk stark naked for about sixteen steps to the loo and I always used to spy over the sheets, pretending I was sleeping, and he was quite proud and he had this huge figure . . . Extraordinary . . . had a bit of a ding-dong later on. And er . . . we'd gradually get up, put

some music on maybe, wander about, have some breakfast
and then upstairs − there was a little staircase to two tiny
rooms above a kitchen. You came into the garden, and then
into the kitchen − that was the first floor. And then above that
there was these two little rooms. One was called the office and
the other was the make-up room where the loo was. And then
the main body of the hall, the mattresses were like in a sort of
in an 'L' shape (like that) and the wardrobe and stuff and the
shoes and the Arabian room at the end . . . and in the sort of
middle of the 'L' shape (over there) was a separate bit where a
woman that lived on the streets stayed, Joyce, and her boyfriend,
so they had that little separate bit. And, er . . . she was lovely −
she was a really nice woman. Somebody had brought her in
because she had nowhere to live and she had this boyfriend
who was a bit thick and much younger − she was in her sixties.

Mark   Did you know much about her life before . . . before
this?

Bette   No, no. She was obviously . . . you could see in her
face she had had a fucking rough time. She was really . . .

Mark   She'd have been born around 1910 or something,
wouldn't she?

Bette   I suppose so, but she was very blind and very much
street-battered by the wind and rain. She was like one of
those gypsies in Portobello.

Mark   And was she, she wasn't critical or uncomfortable or
anything?

Bette   No she was fine, she loved it, and she was only too
pleased to have a fucking roof over her head and everybody
loved Joyce. She was very warm and she had a huge laugh,
very few teeth. A huge laugh!

Mark   And was the commune a political movement do you
think, or was that more like a kind of artistic movement or do
you . . .

Bette   We thought it was very political.

Mark   Right. And were you actually doing political stuff as well?

Bette   Yeah, we were going on lots of demonstrations and things like that in our drag. It was quite scary. You know we used to tend to go out in threes or fours, or sixes and sevens. And if we got . . . we like one time I remember we got arrested, and we had to go to Marylebone, and there were eight drag queens walking together up towards Westbourne Park Station to get on the Tube to go to the court. And when we got there we were being tried for obstruction of the pavement, or some nonsense like that, which they always said it was that kind of thing – they would never say it was a political act. The police would never admit that, or the magistrates. 'And what were you doing there?' you know, and we'd be in our drag and then the court public gallery, it was not that big, but it was full of queens and they all had balloons and they were blowing bubbles into the well of the court, and the police were rushing about and getting very cross. It was a bit sort of mad, pandemonium and we were all off our heads most of the time. I smoked a lot of dope and er . . . took a lot of acid and er . . .

Mark   So how did practical stuff in the commune . . . ?

Bette   Yeah, practical stuff . . .

Mark   Well like eating and . . .

Bette   Well what happened was that you took turns in cooking usually. Some people were lazy and couldn't be bothered. Other people did a bit of cleaning. On the mantelpiece, over behind the record player there were shelves and like a mantelpiece there was a Clarice Cliff teapot and it was rather chipped, and it was rather beautiful and everybody put their money in there. So the rule was you put your money it there, your dole money, or money from the stall or whatever you had, went in there and everybody just helped themselves when they needed it. And it worked quite well for a long time and then somebody stole it – one of the queens stole it and went to Paris, and came back and was totally forgiven because he was young and pretty. (*Laughter.*)

Mark   So tell me, who were the key . . . If we were to do a cast list, who were the kind of key players in there . . . in the commune . . . ?

Bette   Well there were about . . . there was . . . Stuart, me, Michael, Mick Belsten – who's dead, gone now – Nigel who'd been an accountant, Steve was a designer who'd been to art school, and he had this lovely thick long curly hair – it was beautiful – but, er, he's still around. And the women – there were three women – I don't know what happened to them but eventually . . .

Mark   So what were some of the most memorable times actually in the commune for you?

Bette   Well, we'd have these long discussions about our lives, what we were doing, what we were feeling and stuff. Like sort of awareness groups in a way. And some of them would go a bit sour as they did occasionally, but there was a great feeling of euphoria; we were very supportive of each other. We er . . . one night we had a Roman orgy which was fun. We had all these cardboard pillars and stuff and made it all very Roman in effect. It turned into an actual orgy which was very nice, which some people were rather disapproving of . . . I suggested at one point that we all walk around naked when we were in the commune and that was very frowned upon by some people. So we didn't do that – that wasn't adopted as policy. (*Laughter.*) It's funny, it's things that happen. But there was . . . for instance, you'd go up into the make-up room, and one of the great things was the nail polish. Each nail would have a different pattern on it. Some queens would put a nail . . . would be all check – black-and-white check – and the next one might be stripes and so on. So there was time to stop in a way, this was like a kind of cocoon.

Then one morning the police arrived. We were all in bed, you know, and (*laughter*) and eight uniformed police walked in. These great big guys and we thought what's going on we thought . . . and we gradually all got up and we all used to sleep naked, all of us, and we'd get up stark naked and some of us would have a bit of a hard-on . . . 'Yes, what can we do officer?' They'd got all these naked queens surrounding these eight policemen in uniform and they were accusing us of trespassing and all the rest of it, but squatting was quite legal in fact and we pointed that out to them and said that we had every right to be there. Some people were kind of educated or in the law and stuff like that, and they eventually left after about fifteen minutes. It was quite a trip – quite a sight. And so we laughed and hooted about that for the rest of the day.

Mark   So with the commune, do you think . . . did people have a long-term kind of view . . . did they . . . ?

Bette   We thought we were going to be there for the rest of our lives.

Mark   Yeah, OK, did people talk about it? I was just wondering whether people were so in the moment that they didn't think oh we're going to get older and things.

Bette   No, we were absolutely in the moment.

Mark   Right.

Bette   That was a big thing.

Mark   But were you convinced that society would change or was it just about . . . ?

Bette   Yes, yes, I mean we thought that if we kept at it, you know, things would change.

Mark   So if we walked into the commune and said to the group, 'What's going to happen to the world in the next twenty to thirty years . . . ?'

Bette   We'd laugh, say . . . 'Christ knows' . . . I dunno.

Mark   Well it wasn't about planning for the future . . . No?

Bette   There was a guy there called John Church who eventually, sadly, committed suicide, but he was a wonderful actor and he'd been quite successful with the RSC, he was in Scofield's *Lear* and all that stuff, and he dropped out and joined the GLF. And he came and he had a wonderfully sort of Greek/Jewish sort of face, big nose – marvellous face anyway – and he got into drag and we had a wonderful time and all the rest of it . . . and then one day his mother came – she was ninety-seven. She arrived, she was worried about her boy, because he didn't have a father, just had his mother and she came – little tiny woman like a Kathleen Harrison or Katie Johnson. She was very small like that, little hat. And she said

Mother   'Oh hello, can I come in? I'm John Church's mother.'

Bette   And we said, 'Oh fabulous, come in.' She came in and John was in a big long black skirt, nice blouse, flouncy blouse at the top – rather Victorian-looking and he said

John   'Oh Mum.'

Bette   And she came in and she sat down with me, and we made a big fuss of her, cups of tea, bits of cake and all the rest of it. And she sat there and she said, looking round, and we were chatting on and John was chatting on to her. And there was a pause and she said

Mother   'Well, it's all theatre really isn't it!'

Bette   Oh I mean, she was a knockout.

One of the things that happened was some transvestites/transsexuals came down from Birmingham to stay for a weekend. One of them was very tall and they all looked like, or were all trying to look like working-class housewives, you know, only one of them was six foot two for instance, so it kind of looked odd. And it wasn't our sort of drag at all. It was very strange and we just didn't say anything and we chatted about this and that and they wanted to talk about, you know, I dunno, shades of pink slips and whatever. Very kind of like straight, their idea of straight, women, but one of them said there was a problem with the electricity and he immediately skiffed up – we had a ladder there – and he skiffed up this ladder with his spanners and his great big red gloves and he changed all the electricity so that he joined this cable to that cable, these junctions, up this ladder, in his dress, and his wig, and all this rather brown make-up, and he rearranged it so we didn't have to pay for any electricity any more. (*Laughter.*) So he was wonderfully practical. I mean later on people said things like 'Oh the straight trannies never supported us', but they did. That for instance was just one example.

Mark   And what was the attitude of the rest of the GLF to you lot?

Bette   Oh occasionally they'd visit and then there was another commune started up in Bethnal Green, which was called Bethnal Rouge, and that was basically a bookshop – a gay bookshop. There was one in Brixton, the Brixton Fairies, and we'd all go and support each other say in a crisis. Like in the Brixton commune they were getting attacked by schoolkids from this local school. So we all went over there, like at least eight or nine of us, and they had about half a dozen of them living in this little house and at the end of the road there was this school. So they were giving out leaflets in the schoolyard saying about gay people and blah, blah, blah and trannies and drag queens, and er . . . And one day we were there, we stayed there for a few days, and one day sure enough a whole mob of kids starting come up towards the house, right. They were big kids, big heavy brutes and we're all in drag. (*Laughter.*) What we had, we had a plan, they'd come to a certain point and we'd all rush out and charge them. And we did! (*Laughter.*) Roar . . . roar!!! And they ran, they shat themselves. It was so funny! They went back into the fucking school and there was no more trouble after that! And then a few days, a couple of days later we came back and carried on with our thing here, and you could go and stay with them, and they would come and stay with us in Bethnal Rouge . . . (*Laughter.*) It was very exciting.

Mark   And did you miss acting?

Bette   Yeah, and I said one day, I said, 'I've got to do some acting, that's what I am, I'm born to be an actor. (*Laughter.*) So they said, 'Well do some fucking acting.' So I went to French's and I bought twelve copies of *Lysistrata* and I came home and

I handed them out. The women weren't there for some reason at this point except Joyce who was a straight woman.

So we did a reading of *Lysistrata* by Aristophanes.

Anyway, it was a knockout and we read it, and everybody decided to read it as film stars. So one of them was Marilyn Monroe, and one of them was Tallulah, and one of them was Ros Russell, and Ethel Merman, and you know all this stuff and it was great because, you know, it's only women in it and so we all . . . and Joyce read a part and she turned out to be this marvellous actor – incredible! You know I'd had ten, fifteen years in the game before all this, you know, paid-up Equity member and all that and drama school, whatever, and she was just so good. And we pissed ourselves laughing.

Mark   And was there any sense of being part of any international group or network?

Bette   I think with the queens in the commune, by and large, we did think we loved each other, you know. It wasn't a lifelong love but . . . And then you'd get very critical. They'd have these Friday nights where you all had to talk. I remember one time (*laughter*) I shat my box on acid. I was well up there in the cosmos somewhere. This queen turned round and she said

Queen   'We've got to talk!'

Bette (*laughter*)   I was so high I could hardly speak. I said (*laughter*) . . . But you know there was a great emotional thing between us. It was like a new love.

You had to be a bit nutty I suppose, and that was, the thing was that one felt there was nothing left to lose because we weren't accommodated in the world. Nobody in the world really wanted us, we were the sort of remnants, the sort of side plate, you know. We were trying to say, well this is how we live and this is how we want to live, and it was a day at a time. You never thought 'Oh God, what am I going to do when I'm sixty', you know. You never thought like that . . .

And then it gradually diminished . . .

Um . . . I can't remember when the precise moment was but I know it was to do with too many people were into . . . There were some people coming in who were dealers. And there was some heroin coming in, and I'm very straight in a way, you know, I just can't deal with any of that. I can't deal with any of that rather dangerous stuff. And in fact the acid I didn't carry on for that long because once or twice I had a bad trip it scared me so much I couldn't do it any more.

I gave it up really because it got a bit chemical for me. A lot frightened me, you know. Some people were jacking up and some people were obviously . . .

And then when the commune packed up I just thought, oh I've just got to get my shit together somehow. And I got a job here in Powys Square in the playground . . . and I was still in sort of what you might call 'semi-drag', make-up and hair or whatever, and I got a job there looking after the kids.

Well I was working at the playground and Mair, my friend Mair Davies, she's . . . we're still friends. Mair, Welshwoman, she said

Mair   'I've been to see this group at the Oval House, you must go and see them. They're a group called the Hot Peaches and they're from New York and they're doing a show called *The Divas of Sheridan Square*.'

Bette   I went to see this show and it was marvellous. It was done in a sort of . . . like a musical, but all the music was funky rock music. Some of the tunes had been lifted from other people, but mostly they were composed within the group and there was Peggy Shaw, Jimmy Camicia was the governor, and his boyfriend, Ian, they ran the group – they started it and ran it in a loft in New York and they had I think it was two dykes and three queens. Sister Tui . . . they'd found her in the gutter, basically, out of her mind on junk, pulled her together and she was an amazing performer. She had a mouth like a rubber letter box . . . you know. She'd talk like that a lot of the time. 'Oh Babes!'

All the lyrics were all about being a drag queen and being gay and it was very celebratory and there were good songs and good lyrics, good music and good dialogue in the sketches. One was about this queen coming out to her mother and her mother was played by Sister Toohey, 'You mean yer a drag queen!' and her mouth would go like that, 'You mean yer a drag queen!' And Jimmy wrote all the sketches, he and Ian together, they were an amazing creative team.

And they had this tall black queen called Java who sang 'Drag Queen' which is a marvellous song about being a drag queen, and it's an old blues song called 'Beale Street Mama' which was sung by Bessie Smith. And they'd changed the words. It was a wonderful song. She had this glorious black voice. She was about six foot two and all she wore was a boob tube and these very long legs, and these great big shoes like this. So she was coming on seven feet tall really. It was astonishing. And she meant that song. She was heavy into the junk and eventually she was let go from the crew but she went to live in Amsterdam eventually, and went back to America and I think she died but I'm not sure but that night she sang. And I thought, 'That's what I've been looking for!'

Mark   So was it the same night you saw the show that you stayed behind to see them?

Bette   Yeah, and I was in me red jeans, a beautiful hand-embroidered shawl and a lot of make-up and so on . . . Well, we sat around and I went back, and I sat around again and Ian said, 'Look at this queen, she looks fabulous', you know and all that. And I was very much included and then eventually there was this gay woman and she was leaving and I said 'Do you think if I asked to replace you, would you be . . . ?' and she said

Dyke   'Oh yeah, sure dear, that would be good.'

Bette   So I did. I joined the Hot Peaches.

Act Three

Mark Hello I'm Mark Ravenhill. I'm a playwright. In the past few weeks, I've been talking to the performer Bette Bourne about his life. We've divided our conversation into three parts. A life in three acts. Tonight is Act Three. We'd like to read you edited transcripts of our conversations. Ladies, gentlemen and all others – Bette Bourne.

Bette In 1977 I found this book, *Just Myself*, which is about this Australian drag queen who would not answer the question are you a man or a woman. She would say I'm just myself. It was a picture book about this queen's life, lots of dialogue, and it was this interview between her and this journalist. So I got John Church who'd gone back into BBC Radio by that time. Anyway, he decided yes he'd have a go at this. He played the journalist and I played the drag queen.

Mark And where was this?

Bette This was at Hampstead Town Hall. It was our very first Bloolips gig. A one-night stand.

And in the middle of it Diva Dan came on as the maid and she was dressed like a prostitute kind of maid, like a fetish maid. And she was deaf as you know and she came in and she was so wonderfully funny. And she came in and there was the audience and the maid came in and she's like, 'Telephone call for you darling.'

I met him through Gay Lib dances. Oh the Gay Lib dances were fantastic because everybody came in their own home-made costumes, they all came in drag and different sort of costumes. It was lovely, it was astonishing. Beautiful drag. And it wasn't people trying to be women. It was very elegant, in Danny's case absolutely wonderfully elegant. He had a little hat on like a velvet spring. All the deaf queens were in one place in the bar and I saw her and I thought that's amazing. Then a few days later I spoke to Alana my friend. Alana said, 'I want to do a show.' And he said, 'Oh I know that queen, that deaf queen.' So he brought her round then, my kitchen was like a bar with bar stools. And she came round, and sat on one of them there and I'm on the other one there and we talked for three hours it was wonderful, smoking cigarettes like mad and a few spliffs. And I thought this queen has got to be on the stage. And she was doing all this and saw him in the mirror and she's going like that you know, it's hilarious. And I carried on . . .

Mark   And then your second show was . . . ?

Bette   Well I went to the market one day and I found this recording of *The Ugly Duckling* for children read by Jean Metcalfe, ever heard of her? Well she was a very tweedy woman, married to a famous man and she was on television and radio a lot. And she was safe. And she read this story and it was all rather wonderful, and then the duckling went through the forest and all blah blah blah and he was thrown out. So we rewrote it started on Normality Farm. 'All the little ducks go quack quack quack (*singing*) *quack quack quack la LA down on Normality Farm. We don't have doubts or fears, we never have our cares, we welcome you my dears, as long as they're straight and as long as they are square! All the little geese go gobble gobble down on Normality Farm. We're going gobble gobble cos our life is free from trouble! Stick to form, obey the norm, life's a jolly bubble, down on Normality Farm!*'

And it was a huge hit. And we did it in the Tabernacle.

Mark   And how did you find the cast?

Bette   Went round to my mates, do you want to be in a show? We had nine queens. We had Danny, Lavinia, me, and Jon Jon, and there was nine of us.

Mark   And had they had acting experience before?

Bette   None whatever. Only me and Jon Jon. Jon Jon had run a children's theatre group in Australia and had written quite a lot.

Mark   And were you able to rehearse full-time or were lots of them doing day jobs?

Bette Bits and pieces. A lot of them were cleaning flats and that kind of thing. You know, just doing jobs that were a bit elastic. So we'd say well, we'll all get up at eleven or three in the afternoon or something for a few hours and rehearse.

Mark And where would you rehearse?

Bette My flat, well there was a squat above my flat. We're tap-dancing right. (*Singing.*) '*We're in the money . . . We're in the money, we've got a lot of what it takes to get along.*' And I went downstairs after the rehearsal, two hours of this and all the plaster had fallen down in a big lump on my bed in the back room. All the rest had gone and Danny said, 'Bette, Bette, Bette!' We were shocked, everything was a mess. All the dust and dirt from 1867 all over my lovely frocks!

Mark And was it quite easy to get an audience in those days?

Bette Well the word had gone round and there was quite a strong community here then. A writer called Heathcote Williams came and he wrote that play *AC/DC* which was a sort of seminal play in the 1970s. Then he wrote a review of us called 'Bloolips Bare their Brazen Cheeks', cos at one time we all come tapping down and we turn round and we've got bare bums. It was very funny. It was very bawdy and loud. It was very Australian. It was great. It was very strong. They fucking went apeshit because they were all expecting something a bit arty or naff and it was a very strong show. And all the front was benches of kids, cos I worked in the playground and they'd all come to see me dressed as a woman. All these little black kids sitting on the front row, all these different kids. It was great.

Mark And when did you think that Bloolips is going to be something that carries on for some time?

Bette Well Stuart and I went out and had a Chinese meal one night after a show up there and made all these plans, as you do when you're stoned and you're feeling very high. But really I knew it was one step at a time. And Rex said to me, 'Why don't you go to Amsterdam with Danny and see if you can get on at the Milky Way and stuff like that?'

Mark   What's the Milky Way?

Bette   It's a big alternative club. It used to be a milk dairy.
It's huge. So I went over in the fucking snow with Danny and
we tried to get some gigs and eventually we did get a gig for
the summer at the Fondell Park as part of the Festival of Fools
which was a huge organisation that I knew nothing about
until then. And the woman that ran the Milky Way, she came
running up after our gig, we were on the back of a truck
doing our tap routines and we kept chucking the drag over the
side of the truck cos there was nowhere else, so we'd finish a
number and all this drag would go flying out the back of this
truck . . . and then we'd get the next thing on, do the next
number. We'd do a number called 'Bananas', with these huge
cardboard bananas, the Busby Berkeley routine you know. But
with six people it looks completely fucking mad. Hilarious.
Cos we got the bananas and we're trying to get past each
other cos we've got the bananas and it was so small, this truck.
It was no bigger than this carpet.

So we did the show there and this woman came running up
and said, 'We'll book you and we'll do this and this.' And they
did. And they booked us a tour. And that was how we lived
for some years. And eventually after five months one of the
tours finished and I said, 'Well we've got £6,000 in the
handbag.' One thing we never rowed about was the money.
Because I may have told you this before but we always sat
round the table at the end of a gig going, 'One for you, one
for you, one for you, two for me . . . one for you, one for you,'
cos I had the handbag right. We had to have money for petrol
right and everybody thought that was great cos they could see
the money right. The notes. And they would pick up the
notes, put the money in their coat and then fuck off to some
club or other and have a great night. And they'd go to East
Berlin or whatever.

Mark   So how many different incarnations or variations on
the Bloolips was there? Was it pretty much the same people all
the way through?

Bette   Well it started off with six of us. There was Nicky the piano player, Lavinia who'd been a dancer, Danny, myself, Paul and Stuart, who had been an accountant. And Stuart was in from the commune and all that. And these were the people who were very hands-on, who really meant it. And when you have a big success, we went to New York and it was a huge success, we had no idea it would be. We just sent the drag ahead in two great big coffins. We arrived. Everybody went out cleaning cos there was a cleaning agency. Gordon was living there by then and Frank found us all somewhere to stay on people's floors and that kind of thing.

Mark   And what year would this have been?

Bette   That was 1980. A one-night stand in a loft in Greenwich Avenue. And we did the show there. And it was packed. It was like three or four hundred people. They were all sitting on the floor. And the next day George Barteniev, who'd seen it, said to his wife Crystal Field, 'We've gotta have these guys.' Cos I'd been to see them two or three times and she would always say, 'You've got to speak to George,' and he would always say, 'You've got to speak to Crystal.' All this went on . . . then he finally came to see the show and he was (*claps*) knocked out by it. And he booked us the next day. And we had a nine-month run at his theatre.

Mark   What was the theatre?

Bette   It was called Theatre for the New City and next we moved to Orpheum Theatre on Second Avenue. Which was kind of a rung up.

Mark   And what was that show you were doing?

Bette   The show was called *Lust in Space*.

Mark   And did you find over that time that you developed a kind of Bette Bourne persona? In the way that comedians do, I mean was there someone who was Bette Bourne onstage, somebody who was a bit like you, I mean, how . . .

Bette   We were very blurred, the on and the off. I christened
them all. I christened Gretel, Nick was called Naughty
Knickers, Paul was called Precious Pearl, Lavinia was called
Lavinia Coop. I didn't do that name, he did that name, Diva
Dan, and that's it, six isn't it. And Bette Bourne. And different
people came in and out of the group. There was a queen
called Hunter and I called him Bunty Hunter. And we had
another queen called Babs Your Ankle. And another queen
I called Marge Mellows who was a huge tall queen. And if the
tall queens came in very often they'd be rather slouched over,
like this, you know, trying to be shorter with bent legs you
know. And I'd say no, no, we want you tall, we want the
tallest. I want the highest heels you can bear, and the tallest
hat that you can wear and I want you to be the tallest person
in the world. And they were so relieved and so liberated. And
they all came in, I'm telling you girl, with attitude, it was
fabulous. Big, big big tall queens. Cos Vin was quite tall too.
I was trying to do everything opposite in a way.

Mark   In what, opposite to what?

Bette   Well people tried getting into drag thinking that
they'd got to be smaller, that they'd got to be like women and
I would say no tits, no padding, no hips. And it's got to be
white-face. The rest is up to you and they'd do this incredibly
elaborate make-up on top. And they all became really
wonderful at it.

Mark   And what was it about white-face?

Bette   Well I'd got it from the Hot Peaches. They removed
you slightly. It brought up the clown thing, it was very
important.

Mark   So how did you first get to know Quentin Crisp?

Bette   He came to a show at the Orpheum and afterwards
he said, 'Well that was a wild scene.' And I said, 'Did you
enjoy it?' He said, 'Listen to your public they're going mad.'
And they were cheering and hooting and going mad. He
didn't really know what we were about I think. It was such
a strange and anarchic world for him. But he himself was

incredibly anarchic. And he liked us as personalities, he liked us as people. He'd come to the shows and afterwards he would say, 'Oh that was fun!' Or he would say, 'I didn't really understand it.' And after the first time I said I'll come and see you. And he said, 'I'm the most available person in the world.' So I did and Frank and I used to go up there or I'd go up there. But he was a very lovely man.

Mark   So how much time, every year, were you spending in New York?

Bette   We were still getting our shows together here, touring Europe and Edinburgh Festival and all that. But we'd go almost every year from 1980 with a different show to New York.

Mark   And how much did Aids change that scene? Because 1982–3 was when people first – ?

Bette   1983 was when I first heard about it. It was terrifying. People were so sick. People that we knew. It was a very sad time. And . . . oh . . . I started writing them all down at one point. All the people that I'd lost. It was over a hundred. And I just thought I've got to write this down or otherwise I'll forget. And being in the public eye you just meet so many people, and er . . . Vitto died, Martin died, I mean just a long list. Danny died, people in the group became very ill. Nobody was spared. And it was terrible because nobody knew what was going on, how it was happening at first.

There was a lot of sadness in New York. And people say to you to your face, 'I'm gonna die. I'm dying.' And they're like young, twenty-three, twenty-four. What can you say? There's nothing you can do or say. Do a bit of shopping, clean, but you know. That was really . . . But Bill was one of my very greatest, closest friends, Bill Rice, we did a lot of work together and those were his paintings. We were very very close. We used to be in the bar every night. And we used to do shows together. We did *The Importance of Being Earnest* in the garden with all the local queens and couple of women, and we'd do readings, Beckett. He was an amazing person.

Mark   And did you keep in touch with your dad through all of this, how long did your dad live for?

Bette   My dad died when he was eighty-two when I was in America and you know it was so shocking, my brother rang me up bless him and he said I'd rather not do this on the phone but there you are in New York, Dad's died.

Mark   And you were with the Bloolips?

Bette   The old man's died. It was such a shock that I burst into tears. I didn't really have anything to do with him. I didn't like him, I didn't know him really. But I suppose we had got over all the youthful stuff by that time, I just never saw him. But he was my dad, so it had some impact you know, it was like . . . bit of a punch. My mother was upset. She'd been married twice with two other men, but she was still in love with him, she was terribly upset. I remember once I was at her house and he rang up to talk to me for some reason. And she said, 'Is that Daddy? Give me the phone.' And she said, 'Hello, how are you? Blah blah . . . I still love you, you know!' and she gave me the phone back. It's funny. I suppose you never, if you've really loved someone, you don't easily, it doesn't go really, it stays.

Mark   When would you say you were happiest in your life? Is there one day, or one moment when you think you were the happiest?

Bette   Well, it was in Germany in Damstadt . . . I don't know if it was the happiest, but Paul and I, the whole Bloolips were there and we'd done the show and it was a huge success. And we went down into the hall afterwards and they'd cleared the chairs and they were having a disco or whatever it was, and Paul and I were dancing together and we realised how happy we were with each other.

Mark   So when did you start to have a sense that the Bloolips was going to come to an end or that the work of the Bloolips was done?

Bette   Well it was done really when I had this wonderful relationship with Neil Bartlett. He'd been coming to the shows to see the Bloolips for years. Then I saw him doing a show which was called *Vision of Love* which was a solo in Butler's Wharf and Robin did the sets. And it was amazing cos you went in there and it was all pitch black but it was starlit. There had been a storm, and there were great flagstones with dips in them. So there were puddles all over this huge sort of loft on the ground floor. And Robin lit them all, and Neil was stark naked, came swishing through and he'd empty this bag of drag out. All this red net, and he'd make it into all these different shapes for each number.

We did a lot of shows together and it's been very good. I've had a lot of good times. A lot of terrible fights and so on. He's very much a big part of my life.

Mark Would you describe what you do now as drag?

Bette I like wearing drag, I enjoy it. But I don't do full drag now. Unless it's for a part. Now I'm more a sort of disciple of Quentin Crisp. He seemed to strike it right for me. He said a thing that everyone said to him, 'Oh you just want to be noticed,' which I recognised in myself and he said, 'I want to be recognised as a queer.' 'I want to be recognised, that's the important thing.' So he was going . . . I like to be visible. I like people . . . Yeah I like to be noticed. I don't like to be beaten up or insulted but that comes with the territory. But I like to go out visible as much as I possibly can. I don't know why – it's sort of important to me really, because it saves so much aggro. As soon as people say, 'What's your name?' I say, 'Bette.' That's it, it's in the court, it's right in the middle of the court, there's no doubt, there's no questions. Oh yes, she's a queer, she's a queer. That's all, it's quite simple really.

Worst thing is sometimes you go out and you forget, and you haven't got your lippy with you, and you have to go back. That kind of thing. But no, I try to . . .

Mark So if you forget your lippy then . . . ?

Bette If you forget your lippy, that's your kind of warpaint, you see you feel you're not really 'on'. Seems to me that I'm

here so long that being out will become quite important. I
quite enjoy it, I quite enjoy a little bit of danger, a little frisson.

Mark   So you mentioned Quentin in some ways . . .
Quentin, I don't know . . . crystallised for you something . . .
which made a way to be . . .

Bette   Yeah, he had a way of being what he was, and it
wasn't trying to be a woman, it was a man. He was more
effeminate than I am but I don't try and talk 'like that' you
know I don't do all the feminine things because that's not
really me. He was naturally more effeminate.

It's funny, when he died what I missed was not being able to
ring him up in the middle of the night. You know, because
they're five hours behind and I could ring him up and we'd
have a natter, you know. It was fun – I missed that.

Mark   And did you ever talk to him about the actual, the
politics of the GLF and all that?

Bette   No I think he disliked all that because he'd been out
there since the end of the twenties on the street, doing his
thing, and suddenly everybody was doing it. He didn't like
that at all. He wasn't interested in the other . . . And he used
to say things deliberately to upset the queens. You know, he'd
say things like 'Aids is a fad'. (*Laughter.*) You know, it was on the
front pages, 'Aids is a fad says Quentin Crisp', and all the
queens would be up in arms and furious and of course
suddenly everybody's talking about Aids again which was the
point of it in a way, being made conscious of it again, you
know.

But it's very nice when the stallholders in Portobello go, 'Hello
dear, how are you? Got your lippy on I see!' and all this stuff.
And sometimes it's 'You haven't got your lippy on!' They
accuse me. But if I go down there on a Saturday . . . A couple
of weeks ago I went down there and this guy says to his wife,
'Oh he's alright, he knew Mum. He was a good friend of
Mum,' you know. His mother had died and I knew his mother
was quite old when she died and we used to have a sense . . .

yes, I said to him, 'We used to have a few dirty laughs on this corner.' Because with the cockneys it's always a bit rude and a bit cheeky, drag has always been a bit, it's like the drag queens in the pubs in the old days in the fifties all their jokes were about cocks and tits and balls. All very . . . what we call low drag, and that's what they like. Because, especially a friend of mine does it, he does it really well and he goes to these hen nights and the men are not allowed in. There's no men there, they're all working-class women with drinks and fish and chips. And he comes out dressed all in pink, the big pink silvery wig and he really gives it to them, you know! And he does all the filthiest jokes and talks about the men and what their dicks are like and how dirty they are, and all the rest of it. The women love it, he's a wonderful queen. But when he gets out there, he's big! He's very funny because he also brings out terrific anger and aggression him. Been backstage and I've had to say to him, 'I had to go out to the car park for that joke, it was too filthy even for me.'

I suppose for me going to auditions in lipstick, you know . . . Sometimes there is a slight feeling of defiance about them you know, but I enjoyed going for the interview at the RSC in lipstick because this is like considered the sort of . . . the sort of 'top drawer' in a way and my thing was, well this is who I am. That's interesting, that's good. A lot of people are frightened of it.

Mark   And what frightens them do you think?

Bette   Well, it's that I'm well struck in years, I come in, and I present something very strong. And some people are excited by it and book me, and some people are overwhelmed, and don't. You see, other times I'll totally hide everything, unknowingly, because I'm scared, or whatever, I want to work so badly.

Mark   But you don't hide it to the extent that you don't, you're not wearing the lipstick or whatever, so what . . . ?

Bette   Oh when I went to *The Vortex* audition at the Donmar I knew they weren't going to book me with lipstick and I wanted the part very much. So I didn't wear lipstick, I got dressed up as the character. It was slight betrayal of myself, but I got the job and then on the first day I was there in my full slap and Michael said, 'Bette's the only actor I know who comes into the theatre who takes his make-up off and then puts it on again when he's leaving!'

Mark   When you did the Nurse in *Romeo and Juliet* at the Globe was that the same as doing Lady Bracknell, were you playing a woman when you played the nurse?

Bette   No I never really thought about that until I got on. And I got on and the audience accepted me as a woman and as soon as I said the words 'Now, where's my Juliet . . . ' or something, they pissed themselves laughing. And I looked at them. And they pissed themselves laughing again. Then we got on with the scene. So they were saying we know you're a bloke and that was the joke for them. But I didn't approach it like that. In fact in the rehearsals I had a bit of a row because a lot of people were goosing me. I was in my practice skirt, my bits and pieces, and one day there was a dance rehearsal and everybody was there except Tim Carroll, and the dance woman was there. And I said, 'Look I'll just say it once. I don't want anyone touching. Keep your fucking hands to yourselves. I don't want anybody touching me, or goosing me, or fucking around with me. I'm trying to make a person is that alright?' You know. I wasn't going to be the company clown so they could do all that, I was very shocked I said, 'You wouldn't do that if I was a woman. If I was one of the women. You don't do that to the women, you wouldn't do that to the women here. Don't fucking do it to me. Just leave me alone. Let me find my way.' And people came up to me afterwards and apologised, they knew who they were. 'Oh I'm sorry Bette we were just joking, having a lark.' I said, 'Well it's a lark for you but not for me. I'm trying to find an actual person here.' Irrespective of whether it's a man or a woman, a character. What she'd been through. How she walked, how her feet felt, how often she was allowed to sit down or not.

Mark   Do you find now that, I mean, there is a lot more gay theme, there is a lot more, just gay people are a lot more visible? Has that meant people . . . does that mean there's less aggression towards you in terms of the lippy and the . . . Has that changed over the years?

Bette No I think people . . . I was walking to the hospital the day before yesterday and these two guys, 'Look! It's a man! It's a man! It's a man, look it's a bloke, yeah, it's a bloke!' and they were really aggressive and I walked straight between them and on past to my appointment at the hospital. And it was pretty scary and they were completely thrown by it and completely aggressive and angry. No, I don't think things have changed on the street in that way. I think . . . you know . . . try it, anybody can go down the street in lippy and earrings or something and a bit gay-ed up, you know. You'll soon find out how tolerant they are – they're not tolerant at all. Not any more. They never have been, you know. It's different when I go up and down the Portobello Road, it's full of tourists, it's full of people that know me. I'm a local known character, but even then sometimes – this guy, a couple of weeks ago, he was on a scaffold. 'Look at that! Look at that! Call himself a fucking man! Look at the state of you, you fucker!' And for all the world if he hadn't been at work, you know, he'd have come down and hit me. You don't answer back. You have tunnel vision and you go straight ahead. You go where you're headed. It's interesting because the stall-holders on the street, on the Portobello, if they meet me say two blocks off the street they won't acknowledge me, or if they are with their kids they won't acknowledge me at all. They're very London working-class cockneys and it's alright on the street, but it's all bit of a circus on the street but . . . I'm talking big, stocky guys, six foot two with muscles and well struck in years, they'll be really friendly on the street, you know. I said to one of them one day, 'That guy always gives me a heavy fucking time.' He said, 'You want to fucking smack him he's useless.' Two days later, I see the same guy who was telling me this on the street and he wouldn't acknowledge me. He had his little kid with him and wouldn't acknowledge me. They look, and then they look away but they know exactly who you are and in a safe situation to them, men are very, very afraid – men particularly. I was walking down the street one day with this baby, Lorian, in a pram, in drag, and all the women were there and all the men, and all the men are giving me a hard fucking time, and all the women are saying, 'Leave him alone, leave him alone, he's alright, you leave him alone.' They can see I'm doing a job looking after this child. It's very weird, it's very weird.

Mark   And what about now, with your mum and stuff like that? Do you kind of think a bit more before you go and visit your mum, about how much make-up or the clothes you are going to wear, say, when you go and visit your mum?

Bette   She lives in a Welsh village and she's ninety-one and I don't pull any numbers up there – I go very straight. I don't really like going at all because, I don't know, there's a lot of heavy aggression. I was once there in a Tesco's. I literally thought I was going to be slaughtered. No, no, no, that's one of the reasons I don't go there. Quentin used to say to his family over in Jersey, 'I'll come if I don't have to go out.' And he'd come and go to the station, get a cab, go to the house and he wouldn't go out. It's too risky, it's too mad.

Mark   So drag is . . .

Bette   I mean the drag thing was in a way secondary to the subjects that we were doing in the Bloolips, certainly would have been in the Hot Peaches, I was very fearful of real drag queens, very aggressive and frightening. I didn't want to be a transsexual or anything like that. For me the gender thing was fun. It was energising to a degree.

Mark   And if you're honest rather than being politically correct about it, do you still feel any of that kind of discomfort or fear around people having the op?

Bette   Not at all.

Mark   Just because you got to know enough people?

Bette   I know a lot more about it, I meet plenty of people who are into that. I mean it's not a world I'm in all the time but I don't have any fear of it any more. I mean I'm who I am now. I'm seventy nearly, I'm not going to suddenly yearn to be a woman. I've never yearned for that. But I'm a queen. And I love flouncing as much as the next queen.

Methuen Drama Student Editions

Jean Anouilh *Antigone* • John Arden *Serjeant Musgrave's Dance*
Alan Ayckbourn *Confusions* • Aphra Behn *The Rover* • Edward Bond
Lear • *Saved* • Bertolt Brecht *The Caucasian Chalk Circle* • *Fear and
Misery in the Third Reich* • *The Good Person of Szechwan* • *Life of Galileo* •
Mother Courage and her Children • *The Resistible Rise of Arturo Ui* • *The
Threepenny Opera* • Anton Chekhov *The Cherry Orchard* • *The Seagull* •
Three Sisters • *Uncle Vanya* • Caryl Churchill *Serious Money* • *Top Girls*
• Shelagh Delaney *A Taste of Honey* • Euripides *Elektra* • *Medea*•
Dario Fo *Accidental Death of an Anarchist* • Michael Frayn *Copenhagen*
• John Galsworthy *Strife* • Nikolai Gogol *The Government Inspector* •
Robert Holman *Across Oka* • Henrik Ibsen *A Doll's House* • *Ghosts*•
Hedda Gabler • Charlotte Keatley *My Mother Said I Never Should* •
Bernard Kops *Dreams of Anne Frank* • Federico García Lorca *Blood
Wedding* • *Doña Rosita the Spinster* (bilingual edition) •*The House of
Bernarda Alba* • (bilingual edition) • *Yerma* (bilingual edition) • David
Mamet *Glengarry Glen Ross* • *Oleanna* • Patrick Marber *Closer* • John
Marston *Malcontent* • Martin McDonagh *The Lieutenant of Inishmore* •
Joe Orton *Loot* • Luigi Pirandello *Six Characters in Search of an Author*
• Mark Ravenhill *Shopping and F***ing* • Willy Russell *Blood Brothers*
• *Educating Rita* • Sophocles *Antigone* • *Oedipus the King* • Wole
Soyinka *Death and the King's Horseman* • Shelagh Stephenson *The
Memory of Water* • August Strindberg *Miss Julie* • J. M. Synge *The
Playboy of the Western World* • Theatre Workshop *Oh What a Lovely
War* Timberlake Wertenbaker *Our Country's Good* • Arnold Wesker
The Merchant • Oscar Wilde *The Importance of Being Earnest* •
Tennessee Williams *A Streetcar Named Desire* • *The Glass Menagerie*